THE POWER OF NATURE

TSUNAMIS

Arthur Gullo

Cavendish Square

New York

Library of Congress Cataloging-in-Publication Data

Gullo, Arthur.
Tsunamis / by Arthur Gullo.
p. cm. — (The power of nature)
Includes index.
ISBN 978-1-50260-219-0 (hardcover) ISBN 978-1-50260-218-3 (ebook)
1. Tsunamis — Juvenile literature. I. Gullo, Arthur. II. Title.
GC221.5 G85 2015
551.47—d23

Editor: Fletcher Doyle
Copy Editor: Cynthia Roby
Art Director: Jeffrey Talbot
Designer: Joseph Macri
Senior Production Manager: Jennifer Ryder-Talbot
Production Editor: David McNamara
Photo Researcher: J8 Media

The photographs in this book are used by permission and through the courtesy of: Cover photo by JIJI PRESS/AFP/Getty Images; AFP/Getty Images, 4; AP Photo/NOAA, Jacek Maselko,File, 6; NOAA/National Science Foundation File: Superheated molten lava from West Mata submarine volcano.jpg/Wikimedia Commons, 8; File: Pacific Ring of Fire.png/Wikimedia Commons, 10; International Tsunami Information Center/NOAA, 11; sdecoret/Shutterstock.com, 14; daulon/Shutterstock.com, 16; Getty Images, 18; AFP/Getty Images, 20; Dimas Ardian/Getty Images, 21; AP Photo/Ed Wray, 23; Athit Perawongmetha/Getty Images, 24; Maremagnum/Photographer's Choice/Getty Images, 26; Kimberly White/Getty Images, 28; Keystone/Hulton Archive/Getty Images, 30; Central Press/Hulton Archive/Getty Images, 32; Bay Ismoyo/AFP/Getty Images, 34; LCDR Mark Wetzler, NOAA Ship FAIRWEATHER./File: Ship1135 - Flickr - NOAA Photo Library.jpg/Wikimedia Commons, 36; Rhomboid Man/File: Tsunami-dart-system2.jpg/Wikimedia Commons, 37; Todd Gipstein/National Geographic/Getty Images, 38.

Printed in the United States of America

CONTENTS

Waves overwhelm the coast of Minamisōma, Japan, on March 11, 2011.

INTRODUCTION

The monstrous **tsunami** that struck Japan on March 11, 2011 has had long-lasting effects. This giant wave was started by a 9.0 magnitude **earthquake** that occurred 20 miles (32 kilometers) below the surface of the ocean, 45 miles (72 km) east of Tohoku, Japan.

When it hit land less than an hour after the quake, waves with run-up heights (measured from sea level as the water races inland) of 128 feet (206 km) flooded an area of approximately 217 square miles (561 square kilometers) and traveled as far as Sendai, which is 6 miles (10 km) from the shore. More than eighteen thousand people died, most by drowning.

The flooding caused a meltdown at the Fukushima Daiichi Nuclear Power Plant, and forced many countries to question the safety of nuclear power. Germany shut down eight of its older nuclear power plants. Switzerland decided to phase out its use of nuclear energy by 2034. Japan kept its reactors offline, and ordered inspections of those facilities.

The tsunami carried a lot of debris out to sea, and some of it washed up on the West Coast of the United States. In late May of 2014, a skiff landed on the beach at Moclips, Washington that was coated with sea life. The danger posed by this small boat, and other debris like it, is that it carried invasive species that could harm the ecosystems of our waterways.

Debris from Japan washed up on a beach in Alaska more than a year after the deadly tsunami.

Experts from the National Oceanic and Atmospheric Administration (NOAA) said at that time that debris could arrive on our shores for several more years. Biologists instructed people not to touch this debris and worked to collect it quickly to prevent any of these species from establishing colonies.

Tsunamis are the deadliest natural disasters; however, they are always connected to other events. Most tsunamis are started by earthquakes, such as the one that devastated Japan. They can also be started by volcanoes, **landslides**, and meteor strikes. They also can travel long distances and cause harm far from the disaster that started them. The May 2011 earthquake also sent a tsunami across the Pacific Ocean. Its five-foot-high (1.5 meters) wave hit the Midway Atoll National Wildlife Refuge and killed more than 110,000 nesting seabirds.

If Kick 'em Jenny erupts like this underwater volcano near Samoa, it could produce a tsunami in the Caribbean.

CHAPTER ONE
WHAT IS A TSUNAMI?

Four out of five tsunamis happen in the Pacific Ocean, with 86 percent of those the result of undersea earthquakes around the Pacific Rim. This area is called the **Ring of Fire**. Earth's crust is made of giant plates of rock, called **tectonic plates**. There are many **volcanic eruptions** and earthquakes in this area because several of Earth's tectonic plates push against each other around the Pacific Ocean.

However, there is a very active underwater volcano in the Caribbean that could trigger huge waves that could be destructive as far away as the northeastern United States.

This volcano is named Kick 'em Jenny and it is located off the coast of Grenada, south of St. Lucia, six thousand feet below the surface of the sea. It has erupted ten times since

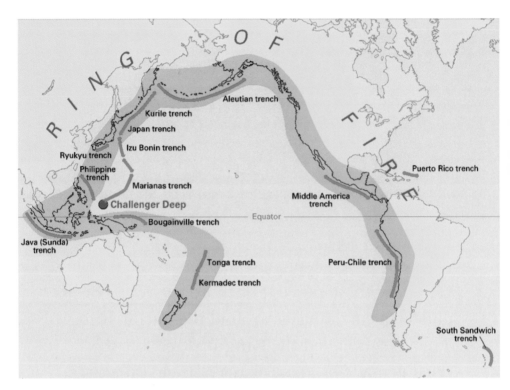

Trenches mark places where tectonic plates collide, producing earthquakes.

1939, the last time in 1990. This is an area at which two tectonic plates, the Atlantic and the Caribbean, meet head-on.

Robert Ballard, director of the Center for Ocean Exploration at the University of Rhode Island's Graduate School of Oceanography and the man who found the *Titanic* on the ocean floor in 1985, has been studying Kick 'em Jenny to learn how volcanoes that are underwater can pose a threat.

Earthquakes

Earthquakes are caused by a sudden movement of the plates that make up the ocean floor and the continents. The plates move about 1 or 2 inches (2.5 or 5.1 centimeters) each year. Over hundreds of years, the plates press against one another.

When plates meet head-on, the lighter plate is forced above the heavier plate. This creates a trench and an earthquake. Tsunamis are created only by this type of earthquake.

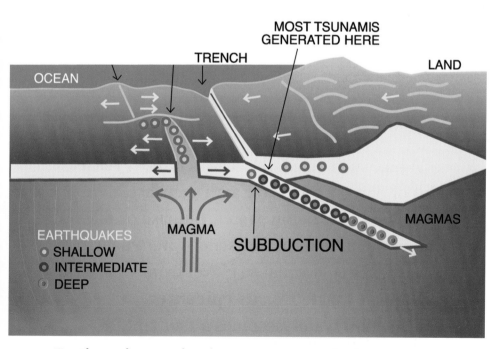

Earthquakes and volcanoes, created where tectonic plates meet, can cause tsunamis.

A tsunami will not be formed if the tectonic plates split apart or slide past each other. It only happens when one plate is forced beneath another.

DID YOU KNOW?

Tidal waves are not tsunamis. They are caused by the gravitational pull of the moon and the sun and are **predictable**. The biggest ones are in narrow bays or rivers near the coast. A storm surge is water pushed by hurricane or typhoon winds. Combined with the rise in the **tide**, surges can cause severe flooding in coastal areas.

When such an earthquake occurs, it releases a lot of energy and the Earth's surface, both above and below water, can rise or fall. Underwater earthquakes send water rushing upward, above normal sea level from where the earthquake started, or its **epicenter**. The rushing water becomes a tsunami.

A tsunami is not just one big wave. It is a series of waves, sometimes called a wave train.

The first of these waves is not necessarily the worst. They can be spaced an hour apart and can cross great distances without losing a lot of energy.

Other Causes

Tsunamis are also created by volcanoes. Volcanoes are openings in Earth's crust through which **magma**—the hot, liquid rock that is beneath the surface of Earth—and hot gases can escape. An eruption happens when pressure builds and the magma and gases are forced out of a volcano. If a violent eruption occurs underwater, it can release a lot of energy. The shock waves made from the release of this energy can cause tsunamis to form.

Many landslides are created by earthquakes. Tsunamis can also be the result of a large landslide or a **meteorite** striking the surface of the water. A landslide happens when huge chunks of land fall into the water.

A meteorite is a piece of rock from space that enters Earth's atmosphere. No one has witnessed a tsunami as a result of a meteorite strike. However, traces have been found of

There is evidence of giant tsunamis started by meteor strikes, but one has never been witnessed.

an asteroid-collision event that would have created a giant tsunami. This tsunami, 3.5 billion years ago, swept around the Earth several times, inundating everything except the mountains and wiping out nearly all life.

Scientists also reported in 2008 that they found evidence of a meteorite strike off Long Island, New York, which may have been the cause of a tsunami that flooded the New York City region 2,300 years ago. There were no earthquakes or volcanoes that could have caused the tsunami.

There are events that can act like a tsunami but are something else. Super Typhoon Haiyan created waves as high as trees in the Philippines on November 8, 2013, killing at least six thousand people and destroying almost half a million homes. The storm surge was measured at seventeen feet in the hard-hit city of Tacloban. With sustained winds of 195 miles per hour (314 kmh), it was called the most powerful storm ever to make landfall.

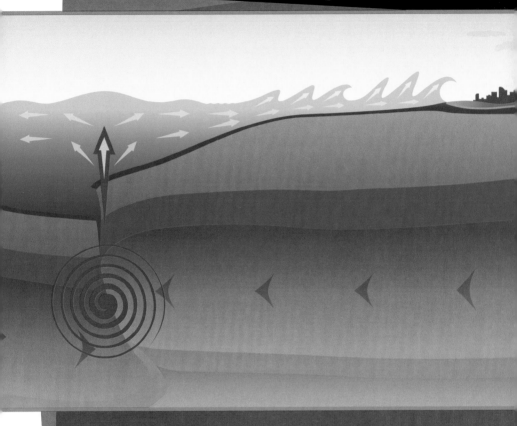

The height of a tsunami wave increases as the water depth decreases.

Tsunami means "harbor wave" in Japanese. The word has been used internationally since 1963. A tsunami can wipe out a harbor, but one could pass beneath you in the deepest parts of the sea and you might not even notice it. This is because it has a far different wavelength than most ocean waves.

Waves are measured in length and amplitude. The wavelength is the distance between two **crests** of a wave. It is a horizontal distance. The amplitude is the height of a wave from the level of the ocean at rest. It is a vertical distance.

Regular waves are caused by wind pushing water at the surface. Under general conditions, they move at 10 to 20 miles per hour (16-32 kmh) and an amplitude of five feet. Tsunami waves are created by an event that affects the entire water column, from the ocean floor to its surface. Their wavelength can be more than 300,000 feet or 56.8 miles (91.4 km) and they can travel at speeds of up to 650 miles per hour (1,046 kmh). Their amplitude can be miles in height but the crest might be only a few feet above the water surface. When that wave hits shallower water as it approaches land, it slows and bunches, reducing its wavelength. The amplitude increases and all of that water builds up to become a large wall.

Homes by the thousands were destroyed in Sumatra by the tsunami in 2004.

The third largest earthquake ever recorded occurred in the Indian Ocean about 150 miles (240 km) from the island of Sumatra in Indonesia. The center of this earthquake, which hit on the morning of December 26, 2004, measured 9.0 on the **Richter scale**.

It raised the sea floor by as much as ten meters along a line estimated at 600 miles (1,000 km). It displaced trillions of tons of rock. Buildings crumbled on the island. People ran for cover and to help those trapped under debris. But the worst damage was yet to come. The underwater earthquake set off a tsunami, sending billions of tons of water moving at speeds of 500 miles per hour (805 kmh) in all directions.

There are two kinds of tsunamis: distant and local. **Distant tsunamis** are created more than 600 miles (966 km) offshore. They are far enough away from land that people have enough time to get to higher ground after being warned. **Local tsunamis** are much more dangerous. They are created 60 miles (97 km) to 600 miles (966 km) from shore.

The tsunami created by the Indian Ocean earthquake was local for the people of Sumatra. The first large wave hit the island less than a half hour after the earthquake did. Survivors said the water made a noise like a freight train. The water surged up to 50 feet (15 m) in some areas, moving swiftly across

The Indian Ocean receded before the 2004 tsunami ripped through Thailand.

The town of Banda Aceh, just 150 miles (241 km) from the earthquake's center, was hard hit by the tsunami in 2004.

beaches and through the city streets. The places most in danger of being destroyed by a tsunami are those within 1 mile (1.6 km) of the shore and 50 feet (15 m) above sea level. A tsunami moves so fast that if you can see it coming, it's usually too late.

A tsunami's waves do not break and curl as normal waves do. Tsunamis often come as rapid floods of water. Tsunamis can also come in the form of a **bore**. A bore is a large, steep wave that looks like a wall of water. It may have a churning, breaking front, but does not look like a typical wave. Bores occur when a tsunami goes quickly from very deep to very shallow water.

Banda Aceh, Sumatra, was the closest major city to the earthquake site. The tsunami moved with such force that trees, homes, cars, boats, and people there were swept away. The waters rushed inland and then back out to sea. Debris caught by the water crushed people. In just fifteen minutes, tens of thousands of people in Banda Aceh were killed.

Over the next several hours, tsunami waves struck at least eleven countries around the Indian Ocean. Waves even hit Africa, about 3,000 miles (4,828 km) from where they had started. The waves killed more than 150,000 people on the first day, and destroyed homes from Africa to Thailand.

Many people believe that animals can sense Earth's geological changes and know when an earthquake or tsunami is coming long before humans do. Hours before the Indian Ocean tsunami, people reported seeing elephants and flamingos heading for higher ground. Dogs and zoo animals refused to leave their shelters. Afterward, very few dead animals were found.

Elephants survived the tsunami, and then helped with the cleanup in Indonesia.

DID YOU KNOW?

Scientists believe the Minoans, who created the first great European civilization in Crete but then disappeared, were devastated by a tsunami generated by a huge volcanic eruption on Santorini in the fifteenth century BCE. This tsunami is believed to be the source of the legend of the lost city of Atlantis mentioned by Plato.

A two-story house in Japan serves as an unlikely docking spot.

Tsunami damages are estimates because the disaster that created them adds to the total. Here are the ten most destructive tsunamis ever recorded.

1. **Sumatra, Indonesia, December 26, 2004; Death Toll, 230,000** Waves reached 164 feet tall (50 m).

2. **North Pacific Coast, Japan, March 11, 2011; Death Toll, 18,000** A lost nuclear reactor added to $235 billion in damages.

3. **Lisbon, Portugal, November 1, 1755; Death Toll 60,000** Waves hit Portugal, Morocco, and Spain.

4. **Krakatoa, Indonesia, August 27, 1883; Death Toll, 40,000** Anjer and Merak were demolished.

5. **Enshunada Sea, Japan, September 20, 1498; Death Toll, 31,000** Homes along coasts were swept away.

6. **Nankaido, Japan, October 28, 1707; Death Toll, 30,000** Thirty-thousand buildings were damaged.

7. **Sanriku, Japan, June 15, 1896; Death Toll, 22,000** Another wave train hit China, killing 4,000 more.

8. **Northern Chile, August 13, 1868; Death Toll, 25,000** Two big quakes affected the entire Pacific Rim.

9. **Ryuku Islands, Japan, April 24, 1771; Death Toll, 12,000** There were 3,137 homes destroyed.

10. **Ise Bay, Japan, January 18, 1586; Death Toll, 8,000** Lake Biwa surged over Nagahama.

(Source: Australian Geographic)

The islands in the Maldives are barely above sea level.

Maldives Spared

The tsunami traveled to the shores of the Indonesian Islands, Thailand, India, Sri Lanka, the Maldives, and as far as Africa and Australia. When the tsunami hit the Maldives, where the highest point is 7.9 feet (2.4 m) above sea level, very little damage was done compared to other affected islands.

The Maldives, which is made up of 1,190 islands, has the lowest high spot of any country in the world. Eighty percent of the country's atolls are less than one meter above sea level. Scientists think that the **coral** reefs around the islands and their low above-sea-level height protected them from the waves. The coral helped to absorb some of the energy of the waves. The low height of the islands, and the depth of the water around them, kept the waves from building into 30- or 50-foot (9 or 15 m) waves as they did elsewhere. The waves there were only one-fifth as tall as the ones that hit Thailand.

That doesn't mean the people there did not suffer. There are 199 inhabited islands in the Maldives, and sixty-nine sustained damage. Of those, twenty were devastated and fourteen had to be evacuated. Electrical and communications systems were damaged. Eighty people lost their lives in the Maldives, but if the waves had been as large as elsewhere, many more would have died.

Tsunamis started by the earthquake near Japan caused damage as far away at Santa Cruz, California.

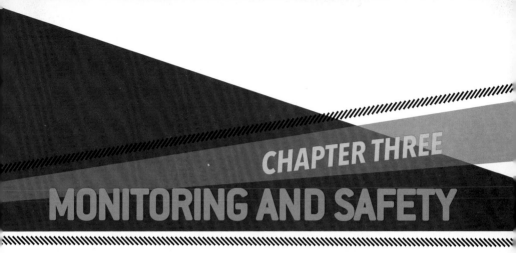

An earthquake in Chile in 2010 produced a tsunami that reached California and caused millions of dollars of damages in harbors. Waves from the tsunami in Japan in 2011 also reached the West Coast of the United States.

Those two events provided researchers with new data that is being used to determine when to send boats out to sea to escape the damage, where to build homes in tsunami flood zones, and what safety features should be included in those new structures.

There are also "playbooks" being designed for communities and harbors on the California coast that will help them set up emergency plans. Tsunamis have been observed one hundred times in California since 1800, and thirteen of them were large enough to cause damage.

Scientists have found the first evidence of a tsunami that hit Half Moon Bay in 1946.

A 1946 earthquake in the Aleutian Islands sent tsunami waves to the California coast.

It killed one person and destroyed some fishing boats. The discovery can help planners know which communities need to be evacuated in the event of a distant undersea earthquake and which routes people should use.

Warning Systems

The nations of the Indian Ocean are just as focused on preventing another tsunami disaster as on rebuilding. Part of the reason that so many people lost their lives in the 2004 tsunami was that there was no effective warning system in place. Since the devastation, people are working to set up a way to warn residents if another tsunami threatens.

Governments, international organizations, and scientists have worked to develop a system to reach the communities on the Indian Ocean. The system includes a network of local communications to quickly warn of a coming tsunami. The Indian Ocean is now being monitored with the latest technology, which watches for the possibility of another tsunami. These technologies have been in use in the Pacific Ocean.

Finding a Tsunami

Seismographs are used to detect earthquakes and other rumblings within Earth. These tools measure the vibrations inside Earth's crust and rate them on the Richter scale. Since only a few earthquakes produce tsunamis, seismographs alone cannot accurately predict when a tsunami will occur. They can rate an earthquake's magnitude so that scientists know when there is a possibility of a tsunami.

Fishing villages bore the brunt of a tsunami in Alaska in 1964.

Much of what the world does to monitor tsunamis was set up after the largest earthquake to hit North America, and the huge wave it caused, occurred half a century ago.

An earthquake of magnitude 9.2 struck southern Alaska on March 27, 1964. Anchorage was about 75 miles (121 km) from the epicenter. The ground in Anchorage shook for almost five minutes, causing avalanches and landslides. Some of these landslides cause tsunamis. The ground around Kodiak was raised as much as 30 feet (9 m) by the subducted plate.

Nine people died in Anchorage because of the earthquake, but 106 died in the tsunamis that swept over fishing villages and across the Aleutian Islands. In Valdez, the wave caused $15 million in damages, made a 4,000-foot by 600-foot (1,219 by 183 m) section of land fall into the sea, and killed thirty-two people. The village of Chenega was destroyed and twenty-three people died. The biggest wave, 219 feet (67 m), was recorded at Shoup Bay, where one person died.

The tsunami killed eleven people in Crescent City, California, four on the beach at Newport, Oregon, and one at Klamath River, California.

The earthquake led to the development of the Alaska Tsunami Warning Center and eventually to the NOAA Tsunami Warning Centers. These monitor hazards from tsunamis worldwide.

Early warning systems are being improved in Indonesia.

Scientists also use **bottom pressure recorders** to monitor the oceans. A bottom pressure recorder on the ocean floor measures the water pressure every fifteen minutes. If something unusual is detected, it will measure every fifteen seconds to gather more information.

Buoys are often used to measure conditions in the deep sea. A floating buoy sends its own data and data from the bottom pressure

Hawaii averages about one tsumani per year and a severe one every seven years. The biggest tsunami to hit Hawaii happened in 1946. Waves that reached the coast of Hilo Island soared to a maximum of 45 feet (13.7 m). The Hilo waterfront was destroyed, and 159 people in Hawaii were killed.

recorder to a satellite. The satellite sends the information to watch centers around the world. This system is called the **Deep-ocean Assessment and Reporting of Tsunamis (DART)**. It is used now in both the Pacific and Indian oceans.

Sealevel and tide gauges are also being used to detect tsunamis in the Indian Ocean. These **gauges** measure the sea level and tides at the shore. They were in the Indian Ocean before the 2004 tsunami, but did not send data regularly enough to be useful. These gauges have been improved so that they now send data in real time to tsunami centers in the region. Scientists in tsunami centers now learn of changes as they are happening. The gauges are being fitted with solar panels so that they will work during a power failure.

The United States Geological Survey has been developing an Earthquake Early Warning System for the West Coast to give residents there more time to escape a tsunami.

Buoys collect and transmit data to satellites, as shown at right.

Tsunameter Mooring System

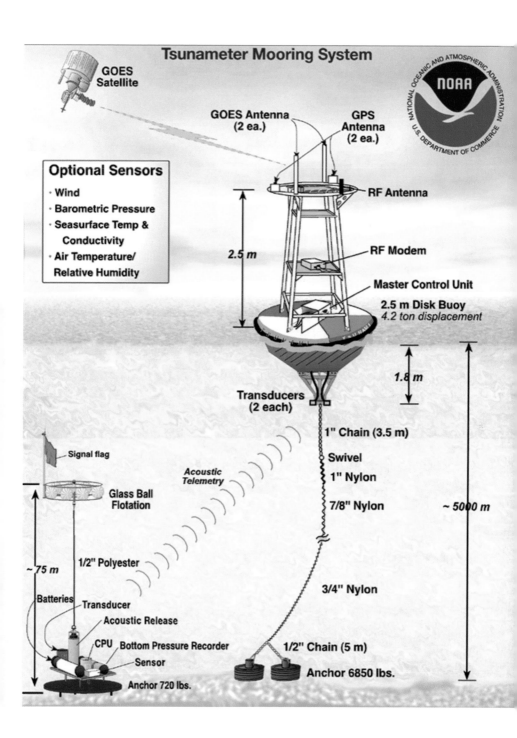

GOES Satellite

GOES Antenna (2 ea.)

GPS Antenna (2 ea.)

RF Antenna

Optional Sensors
- Wind
- Barometric Pressure
- Seasurface Temp & Conductivity
- Air Temperature/ Relative Humidity

2.5 m

RF Modem

Master Control Unit

2.5 m Disk Buoy
4.2 ton displacement

1.8 m

Transducers (2 each)

1" Chain (3.5 m)

Swivel

1" Nylon

7/8" Nylon

~ 5000 m

Acoustic Telemetry

Signal flag

Glass Ball Flotation

3/4" Nylon

1/2" Polyester

~75 m

Batteries

Transducer

Acoustic Release

CPU Bottom Pressure Recorder

1/2" Chain (5 m)

Sensor

Anchor 6850 lbs.

Anchor 720 lbs.

People in Hawaii must always be watchful
of tsunamis.

What Do You Do?

The states at highest risk of experiencing
a tsunami in the United States are Hawaii,
Alaska, Washington, Oregon, and California.

People in low-lying coastal areas in these
states should be prepared for one because
they will have as little as a few minutes to

escape to higher ground after an earthquake in the Pacific Ocean. The Red Cross says early warning signs are a strong earthquake lasting twenty seconds near the coast or a sudden rise or fall of water on the coastline. Here are steps a family can take to increase their chances of survival.

- Know how high above sea level your street is and the nearest place with an elevation that will keep you out of harm's way.

- Teach your family an escape plan for reaching that higher ground.

- Have disaster supplies, including a flashlight, batteries, a battery-operated radio, a first-aid kit, and emergency food and water, ready in easy-to-carry containers.

bore A kind of wave that is large and steep and looks like a wall of water.

bottom pressure recorders Devices used to measure the pressure of water at the ocean floor.

buoys Floating markers in oceans or rivers.

coral A substance found underwater, made up of the skeletons of tiny sea creatures.

crests Tops of something such as a wave or a hill.

Deep-ocean Assessment and Reporting of Tsunamis (DART) A system used to monitor oceans and detect tsunamis.

distant tsunamis Tsunamis that are more than 600 miles (966 km) from shore.

earthquake A violent shaking of Earth, caused by a shifting of the crust.

epicenter The area directly above the place where an earthquake occurs.

gauges Instruments for measuring water height.

landslide A sudden slide of earth and rocks down the side of a mountain or a hill.

local tsunamis Tsunamis that occur between 60 and 600 miles (97 and 967 km) from shore.

magma Hot, liquid rock found beneath Earth's surface; when above ground, it is known as lava.

meteorite A piece of rock or metal from space that enters Earth's atmosphere at high speed and does not get burned up in the process.

predict To say what you think will happen in the future.

Richter scale A system of measuring the strength of earthquakes.

Ring of Fire An area on the outer rim of the Pacific Ocean where there is a lot of volcanic and earthquake activity.

seismograph An instrument that detects earthquakes and measures their power.

tectonic plates Large sections of Earth's crust that make up the continents and seafloor.

tide The constant change in sea level that is caused by the pull of the sun and the moon on Earth.

tsunami Very large, destructive waves caused by an underwater earthquake, volcano, or landslide.

volcanic eruption A forceful explosion of magma and gases from a volcano.

FURTHER INFORMATION

Books

Birmingham, Lucy, David McNeill. *Strong in the Rain: Surviving Japan's Earthquake, Tsunami, and Fukushima Nuclear Disaster.* Houndmills, Basingstoke, Hampshire, UK: Palgrave McMillan, 2014.

Caruthers, Margaret W. *Tsunamis.* Danbury, CT: Franklin Watts, 2005.

Henderson, Bonnie. *The Next Tsunami: Living on a Restless Coast.* Corvallis, OR: Oregon State University Press, 2014

Thompson, Jerry. *Cascadia's Fault: The Coming Earthquake and Tsunami That Could Devastate North America.* Berkeley, CA: Counterpoint, 2012.

FEMA for Kids: Tsunami

www.fema.gov/kids

Learn about natural disasters, including tsunamis, and how to prepare for them on this Federal Emergency Management Agency website. Also, see dramatic photos of tsunamis and play a tsunami-related game.

National Geographic

environment.nationalgeographic.com/ environment/natural-disasters/tsunami-profile/

Read stories, watch videos, and take quizzes about these killer waves and what they do to our environment.

NOAA National Weather Service

www.tsunami.gov

Get the latest information on tsunami warnings, advisories, or watches.

Pacific Tsunami Museum

www.tsunami.org

This website provides information on preparing for and surviving a tsunami, and tells the tale of a family that lived through one of the biggest ever.

Woods Hole Oceanographic Institute Tsunami

www.whoi.edu/home/interactive/tsunami/

Watch this interactive guide that can teach you about these disasters and maybe save your life.

INDEX

Page numbers in **boldface** are illustrations.